FLASHBACKS IN MY CASSETTE

ANUSTHA PAL

Copyright © Anustha Pal
All Rights Reserved.

This book has been published with all efforts taken to make the material error-free after the consent of the author. However, the author and the publisher do not assume and hereby disclaim any liability to any party for any loss, damage, or disruption caused by errors or omissions, whether such errors or omissions result from negligence, accident, or any other cause.

While every effort has been made to avoid any mistake or omission, this publication is being sold on the condition and understanding that neither the author nor the publishers or printers would be liable in any manner to any person by reason of any mistake or omission in this publication or for any action taken or omitted to be taken or advice rendered or accepted on the basis of this work. For any defect in printing or binding the publishers will be liable only to replace the defective copy by another copy of this work then available.

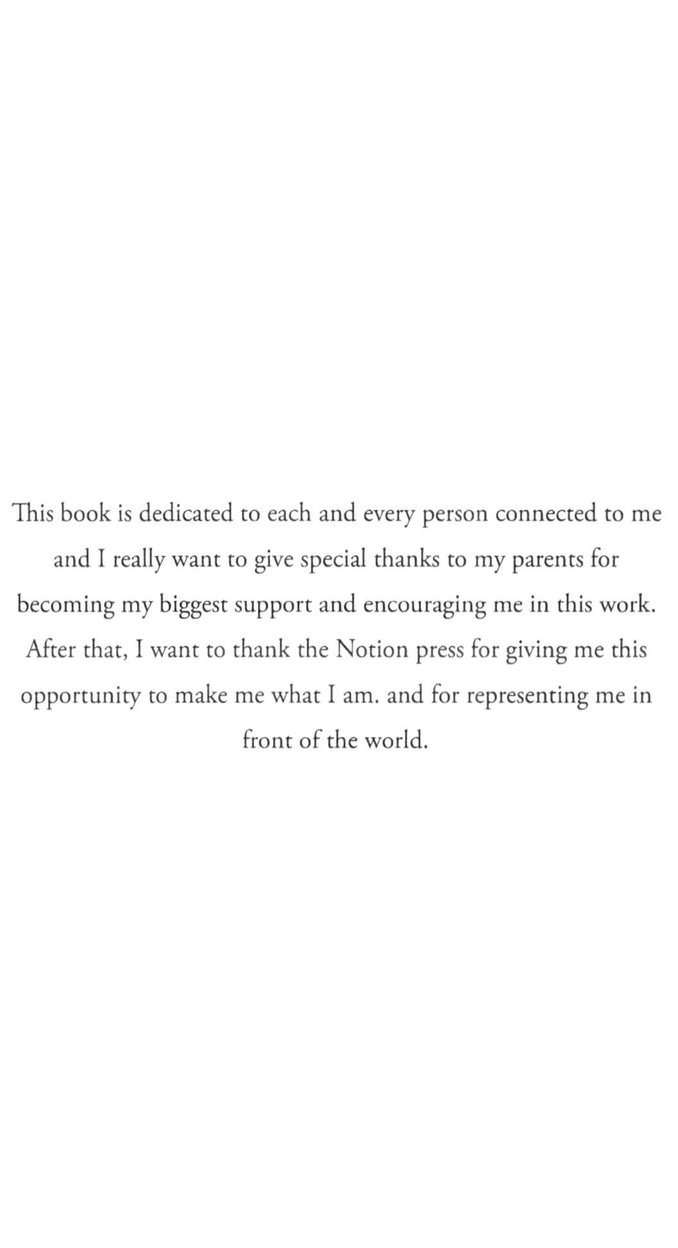

This book is dedicated to each and every person connected to me and I really want to give special thanks to my parents for becoming my biggest support and encouraging me in this work. After that, I want to thank the Notion press for giving me this opportunity to make me what I am. and for representing me in front of the world.

Contents

Contents

Foreword

The author of this book Ms Anustha Pal, started writing books when she was 19. she took her graduation with a Bachelor of technology in computer science, which is too Far from writing but she define her writings and poetry at that time making her publish her thoughts and vision in the form of a poetry book. Her parents and people around her inspire her to write what she feels. She inspires people around her by being a beautiful Poet. she wrote amazing books - Scars, Door to my soul etc that are too interesting to Read.

Preface

This book is a collection of wonderful feelings which are not easy to tell or express. But we all belong to this. According to me, feelings are something very hard to resist. Like if you are sick so you have so if anybody asks so you directly tell them that you are sick, but behind that many feelings are hidden which are difficult to express. Which only our soul can feel. I come out with this book to take you on a soulful journey.

The feeling of love contains thousand unexplainable feelings which are like different shades of single colour of love. So took you deep inside the world of feelings, through my poetries you can feel relaxed mentally. basically, I love to write in between the lines which took hard to understand but that is the key to take your soul too deep and intense. I hope you all enjoy reading this book.

1. Story of everyday

Blush on your face,
Let come into my space,
Street crowded waiting for
One plate of momo,
People fall for its taste.
Just look over the scorching sun,
Making body tan in summertime.
Far from woods these markets have
Women in red, yellow and green
Some also wear light pink.
Everybody loves the spring
but summer Is too hot to handle.

In spring under the warm sunlight
your shadow chasing me.
I ask her to stop chasing me but
Like my dog, he follows me in every
Narrow Lane.
Then I see a canopy and my shadow
Disappear somewhere.
This warmness has some cozy
Feeling that I use to breathe.

Now it's time for sunset and
the weather cools down,
And when I see orange sun and
Yellow moon together that was
a beautiful Feeling of every day.

2. In your sphere

In the world of yours
Gratitude that you gave to me,
The days that you spent for me,
All are under the sea of devotion.
For raise, praise and grace
the peices in me need a break
For the small world that diminish
And lost in space.
life is a 3d animation to bring
Twist in Cartoon characters.
Similarly I try to bring life to
words.
Your imaginations sound In
my words,
I m the goddess of my small
Universe.
In the solitary of your, I am
a sound that blaze and roar.
You are the gratitude that make
Me sure I am someone special
In this big world of yours.

3. Lost moments

Story of moments
Very small I even can't count
Moment end in lapses and
That mysterious sounds.
Besides the river that lumbering
Sound, sofisticated and unique
There time is still but moments
have a great count.
Sometimes a home full of jolly,
Sometimes a desert of sorrow.
We have clock that count time
And there are peices of moments
That hold my highest climbs
But there is no clock to calculate the
Moment i live for mine.
Time that we spend with close ones,
The love that moment extract within
Our lifetime.
They change value of moments into a
Great time.

4. Sounds

The sounds that awake me
from my bed.
The sounds that want me to
feel better than worse.
Sound that sleep in my head
and make every morning best.
Up from the stairs catching
The ball is thrown By my brother,
Catching Sound crunchy
that knock my head,
Something yummy mom
Left in the cupboard.
Sound of the beetles
On the grassy Nights,
Sounds of the refrigerator in
the summer,
Slurping cold water into
The mouth
Choas that making us
feel Delight.
Sound of anklet of my
mother when she Came,

Heavy sounds when
She scream,
But one day they all vanish
with me.

5. Gathering and talks

Gatherings are great
But they hurt.
Talking Makes you
feel cool but Sometimes
stuck.
You have small talks
And beautiful gestures,
but you realize in that
conversation You are
losing your worth.
Most of the time you
Thought of being a most
desirable person but you flee.
Some gatherings are Hazy.
Some topics of the discussion
Are political,
Few topics are social-based
On discrimination law and family.
Many people go for devotional
Topics for search for god and faith in
Somebody.

Some talks are never ending
And gave us lots experience
And memories.

• 8 •

6. Argue

Argue on your point if
It is valid,
Otherwise, delete your
Opinion from the conversation
And just agree.
Getting to know about
Talks that people talk over,
Some people argue for a
Price of burger that famous
People ate that night.
Some people argue that they
Have seen god at midnight,
Some people talk about the
Beautiful gowns that Diana
Was wearing,
Few are telling the discovery
That they have made.
I am impressed by your
presence and your great
Talks,
But Some arguments are
Just a waste of time.

Some talks sound frustrating
To my soul.
Then You come with
Your cute words,
you spell them out
Like a bunny.
Your expression pause my
Mind and I come out of arguement
And feel peace with big smile.

7. Honesty

Fishing out all the things
I have
I determine to one point
That being without honesty
what my Life is ?
You are making funny faces
But mind need some separate
Spaces, but in the last honesty is
My real place.
You go out on an evening to
Search existence of your name,
There are a lot of fake people
But if I go with them my existence
Become fake.
Figuring out the points that
This world target on you,
You draw and run in your own
Lanes,
Sing for your victory in your own
Pace and tell this world honesty
In your give blessing that you give
each and everyday.

8. Pillow

Watching dreams your my sleep,
Years ended but we never reach,
But there are some anecdotes my
Pillow catch in my dreams.
Carrying all the heavy luggage
of memory of my head,
Healing my back, making me
Feel the comfort and talk to my anxiety
For almost every day.
Pillow asks me to dream
All the possibilities in next week,
Pillow hold the tears of my sad prose
She listen my rotten stories on rewind
And hold me even in bad moods.
But still my pillow never leave
She camly say you are a blessing
Not a freak,
And tell good days are waiting
for smiles And laughs,
Just set yourself free.

9. Untold

In chasing the evening
With Juice and lemonade.
Under the delight of your
Love, I am becoming a grenade.
Sometimes I don't have enough
breathe To hold in my lungs
Even it's hard when some people
Left in the middle of the Road
For months.
Journey investigate the files that are old
Memory is a precious gift to rewind
To the old roads.
I can't even bury my dream for the opinions
That you have told
My major life ends with your love
That's how my story is untold.

10. New starting

When all the feelings,
Cover up you with emotions
Brave soul become mushy and
Get you draw your dreams from
Pastel colours.
When you look over in the sky
And it start to rain,
When you loss focus and nervousness
And grasping what you love,
A dream become reality and change your
Lonely mind.
The decision run fast in the direction
That is right
When Fortune have faith in you
That's a lovely side.
I leave all that pain in my old
Eyes
And i think this new world is better for
My life.
Cause there we always have two lives
The second one start when you
Realise you only have one.

11. Whispering sounds

A sound whisper in
my head eternally,
I have never heard
this sound before but
I can't imagine my life,
without this sound.
Some people laugh
and make fun of
That whisper sound,
They confuse me
that i am cracking
jokes Or they are just
laughing on my wounds.
Some intuition say
don't focus on
The thought of people
who are too creep,
Just run only for
those sounds which
Make you feel
responsible and happy.

12. Aimless

I am scampering the bubbles
In the air,
I lay under the sky every night
For counting the star,
I m doing things that are silly
To be a careless freak all the time.
But time tells for chasing all the dreams
You have to make the identity of a unique kind,
make sure you can survive,
And then One day you are on
the highest peak And fly.
Bringing out all the ease at one side,
Rock on a Stunning stage without aimless
Eyes,
Life is running track, a fight for food and
Stay, first ensure that you have a ceiling on your
Head.
In my shelter, there is a hole in the ceiling at
One side,
Rain come and fall ? on my eyes,
Also fall on the floor and i put bucket to
Save my floor from getting wet in midnight,

At that time i realise my father's worth.
So i drop me for the peices of work like
A rain drop,
Sometimes everyone try to let me down,
In all that part i decided to change
My vision from aimless parts,
On building castle for my life goal that
I once lost.

13. Villan

Villan of every story,
Always have a reason for misleading
The glory,
Frankly speaking, I am sad from your
Dark theory.
My vicious crime has a mythical knife
That stabs you in my every scandal story.
Reading all the rough thoughts that you
Think when you think of me.
You always put your efforts to let
Me down,
That's the reason for thousands of
Murders and crimes.
You always try to give me a new hell
All the time,
Where my voice screams and there is
No one to listen to my sad rhymes.
But things that I want to tell you
From the red colour of my blood,
That I am gold medal that people
Get after the victory,
I am the intense emotion everyone

Feel when they try to heal,
A sweet catchy voice that people
Love to hear,
A hilarious wind into hair that makes
People feel the love with an emotion of
Rainy breeze,
I am the confidence of our hearts that
Others try to break,
This is what I am made up of.
Now you are with red scoundrel eyes
But still, I have no fear in my eyes,
And I will fight Because Villan always have one negative point
And heroes have one positive point so
This is how they always make a difference
God will identify and they help the hero
For goodness and that's how Villan die.

14. Blame game

The blame game is on,
in the supervision of thoughts.
We hear what heart and
other people are saying,
Remembering all the events
That is going on,
For our safe zone we went for a
Blamegame.
We usually believed in easy things,
But telling us we are wrong is hard to
Admit, that sometimes lands us in
Some dark place.
Coming out of it is not easy and we
Reframe, that's how again we are on a
Blame game.
We blame our society and people for
The moments that we are unable to enjoy,
We blame sourounding for not being happy,
And that suffering heart feel it is time for
Blame game,
We are not accepting the facts that
Are critical, we are the master of our

Own destiny.
We need to soften our thought and
need to rethink and restart it all,
Stop blaming others for your sadness
Try to flash them out and put small smile
On your face for some brightness.
Because if you again choose a next blame
Game so your confused heart will regret
And nothing admirable left.

15. Altruistic

Into a red hut and green garden
I know a girl altruistic and kind,
When people fighting for their
own life,
Some people just making efforts
To make you feel fine,
When in this world people
Find hard to help,
Altruistic bring flowers to others
When she is in a tough time,
Then also she first thinks of you
In the meantime.
She sometimes feels hard and having
Pain in her heart,
But still, she fights for others every time
She is out of my dimension and i am unble
To understand this psychology of their
Mind,
Altruistic have sweet and simple smile,
Her empathy, love and passion make her
Unique in my eyes.
To all the atruistic people who feel sad

This time,
I accept you are most beautiful people
In this world who bring humanity on
The Great place of great divine.

16. Patsy

Out for a walk taking one
Step forward,
When people see her she
Grin and Make them
feel humorous
People phrase that Stacy
Is a woman with character
Sweet and shy,
She completes her projects
Before deadline.
But Stacy never tell her that
Her grace makes her life hard,
It's not good to be sweet every time.
Within Adulting she learns more
And help more,
But she never realizes that her identity
Is framed as a helper.
Wise and clever standing at her end,
Just waiting for their next manipulation.
Everyone uses her like a machine
learning data,
Good people are once in a blue moon

In her life,
She has a lot to tell but she hide it.

She think she is stacy and pure,
And helping is her goal,
But i think she need to rethink.

17. the Soldier

The story of a old man
Black eyes, blue shirt and
Grey pant,
With good features and tall
Height looking
gorgeous with my aunt.
A man showcasing his life
Infront of people by holding
Car keys and a dog.
He is telling about the bravery
That scored in his life.
He is cracking his luxury infront
Of people and shining.
Some people ask him other things
That are different,
So he clearly tell he doesn't waste
His time on tiny small things.
He sat on the table and start discussion
But he start and end only on him.
His obsession seems very different,
He is very confident about what he
Is saying,

He looking very tough and strict,
He is perfectly following his life according
To rules,
He cross the maze with grace
And his grave is packed with national flag
And there life end but their story will never
Stay.

18. Trigonmetry

I am a triangle with three different
Angles,
My one angle is talkative, second is
explorer And third is social,
The first angle that my eye has seen
tell to see the world from different
View and know the geography of earth and
People around us.
When I come into this zone my life is crazy
I talk to everyone very easily.
On the other angle, I am shy, sweet and
Silent like an innocent girl enjoying her own
Comapany.
At that time talking is not easy,
I am just observing things and watching
The beauty of silence,
To be alone is the greatest thing that i feel
And in the parties sitting alone and confusing
Everyone about the character of me.

And the third angle is being weird that
Is hidden inside the closet of my heart,

That I express to my small family
Where i can express stupid, annoying
Any kind of things,
That almost happen barely
But these three angle have different
Degree.
But still when i sum up the two angles
In me i form ambivert character angle in me.
The ambivert angle is greater than the angle
That is third weird angle in me.
This is all about my trigonometry.

19. Serenade

The moments that make great
Stories.
The eyes that don't blink after
feeling comfort zone in your eyes.
When you don't need hands to
create gesture, your eyes are
Enough.
When you feel delighted from someone's
Embrace and feel beautiful with grace.
That means you love that person from
All you have, so now become more risponsible
Fought for the promise that is from one heart
to another heart, even if the door of the world is getting close for
you.
Making promises is easy but standing on
Them and efforting and all that stress that
Your face leads you to greatness.
These sphere of memories has
Corners that will hurt you and also
Have sound that make you feel ease
Within this peace.

In our hearts the love that we keep,
That let us know there we don't have any
Boundary.

• 31 •

20. Healing papers

My smouldering soul burning with the
Sensation of flame.
I need some pure vibes and graceful
Rain to feel serene and beautiful dame.
Cattle grazing in the farm and terrace
I love this kind of simplicity, i don't blame.
Lifting life and turning pages from these
Days to those days,
But you need to show compassion to leave
The legacy behind of your name.
This life give all of us some burning pains
But leave them and feel delight in the nature
Frame.
Stop running for this undivine universe, people
And fame,
Your presence and peace of mind is greater than
Anything in this life of game.

21. The art gallery

I was moving through
an art gallery,
And I saw a portrait that
smell like
A garden full of roses,
It sounds like a melody that
my ear Love,
An old song that I heard for
the first And fallen love with.
I never knew that
continuously running
The world has time for this,
but that feeling has flinched.
I ran back the home,
With some wince.
I see the portrait again,
I m feeling nostalgia from
Where I start,
Someone was lying within
This art,
The greatest artist with
Whom,

my eyes want to meet.
This dark life finds some bright
Pictures,
That always heals.
I woke up early in the
morning and take My meal,
I saw that painting in my
imagination again and again
Like my room has a big wall
Of dream,
My heart only knows what
I have seen,
Because I am so obsessed so
I take back me to the art gallery
To relive the moment.
Every time I see that painting,
I relive my childhood and
Back to the bin of memories.

22. Young soul

I m the words of a
Young soul,
We are our gritty and
Harsh pathway
Shiny things attract to
Our soul.
Bad things pull us to
Bad decision,
Our lives look soft but
Have some parts that are
Rough.
Our minds bleed with words
That compares us from others.
But we accept it although.
We are here to make our place in
Hearts and minds,
We believe in stability but growth
Is overwhelming kind.
Glowing growing glamorous grey
Lives,
We love fame even in flames.

life is book with turning pages,
Do something that remember by
Ages.

• 36 •

23. Untold & Unsold

I am Novel of Anustha,
Never written never told,
Look like i am a big secret
That she holds.
Her eyes has a dream to
Be bestseller,
She want to express her
Soul and what she is overall.
She taught her learning
Her aim is too broad,
But when she comes to
Me feel tired and bored.
It's like i am not her
Priority, out of the list of
The goals.
In sake of finding best
Story follow your soul.
I am not loosing the hope,
One day come when i am
In the book that highest sold.

24. The dance floor

In the city of Kolkata
inside a big palace,
There is a game of dance.
Folklore is the theme and rules
Say if you stop then you
Are out of this dance.
When the dance start
Everyone is in good shape,
But abruptly rain started
and it becomes arduous
To catch the move and
dance.
Some dancers vent their
Form and due to slippery floor,
They fall on the grass.
Now the rain has done their work
And the sun begins to rise,
But they heat a lot that melts
Some dancers and they dehydrate
And fall.

After that sun hide behind

the clouds,
And it becomes too dark.
unexpectedly mist cover
all the palace,
And cold wind coming from
all the sides.
Some dancers catch a cold,
they start To sneeze and
now only rare dancers left
On the dancing floor.
But even after that deliberately,
all the exhausted People fall
On their knees,
One after other leave the floor
Gradually
and the ultimate dancer who
Have the greatest will
is Standing on the floor
And chase the game.
Till the last his survival make him
The winner of the game.

25. Purpose

There are many things
that you want to achieve,
There are a lot of things
that you are good at,
But life always gives you a
purpose To live for.
Choose everything that you
Love but never leave your
Purpose in the halfway.
Never go for the opinions
that are in others' heads.
Never follow others' destinations. it will kill you With stress.
Life is not just a race to run
It has relations, emotions,
adventure,Money and fun.

There are many things
you are good in,
But purpose is some
things that gives your
big reasons.

If you run after all the things,
life will not admire,
But living for a purpose makes
You feel worthy in the end.

26. Soulmate

Everyone loves to meet moly
In me,
She is pretty and puts glory in
Me.
She always searches me in my
Tired days,
She is always ready to talk to me
in my empty space.
She loves to search for me in the
Good and nostalgia vibes.
She sometimes doesn't have time
So she lends one ear at home,
Because she always wanted to
Know,
She wants to be my support
System although.
Attach with subconscious
Mind although.
She loves to watch me but
She never admit her love
Its look like her love is
unintentional Like a mother.

She is part of my soul
that Know what is best for me,
She will be there in my heart if
There is no one for me.

27. Bread crumbing

In the age when Ronny is too
Young,
He has some feelings for
Daisy Doofenshmirtz.
But he doesn't know she
Will bread crumb.
He makes a bundle of all of his
Confidence and messages her
Hi for the once.
Daisy doesn't have faith in him
But she messages back for fun,
She feeds him a message after all
The day and then leave him like
A Piece of shit again.

After that, she call him just to
Show that she was there

But actually she stay away from
Him one by one.
She just trying to attract,cause
Her physiological self call her
To do so,
She showed ronny how close she is,
But in actual there is nothing more
Than intuitions,
From daisy he consider everything
Is a beautiful truth.
She make a linear path on the
Curvy life road through the words
And phone calls.
Ronny found it intresting so he
Started running behind her.
But in the end he is in the woods
Alone with negative vibes and sad
Prose.
She leave him alone in the woods
And hansel him, nothing more than
Sad songs left for him,
This is about bread crumbing.

28. Stranger again

Some strangers turn into enemies,
Some start their love, perhaps they
All belong to each other so they give
Eachother best.
Some stranger giving birth to a stranger,
Some strangers lying in the graveyard,
Some strangers playing the guitar together.
Some turn into family and some into
Closest one.
Some turn into good and some into
a piece of worry.
Some stranger brings a tear to your
Eyes,
Some fell with the tears of your
Eyes.
Same goes with the stranger sitting
On the park bench,
Some wait for the desired stranger till the end
In this story of a stranger some stay for a
Moment and some for the life time.
Some become important part of life.

If you keep them in heart relations grow
In days
But if you leave them from your they become
Stranger again.

29. Self complaining

Complaining every time,
everywhere and to everyone.
Stop!! Stop!! Stop!!
A life which is sweet and short,
Complaining makes the life quart.
It's ok if you are not flawless and white,
but you can vastly grow
In months if you are on the path
which is Right.
Many of us complain that
we don't get things that are bright,
It is not necessary to serious
about every point that you
learn worldwide.
Getting everything in one life
depend on uponYour a bucket list
You made it at midnight.
reaching milestone don't have
shortcuts to reach,
First you have to learn and teach.
Sometimes life is lonely and sad
But it doesn't mean life is ugly and quite.

May be on the next node you get something
Unbelievable for which you are meant.
But complaining from everyone make you
Look like sad story which other people
Don't love and you also feel awful about yours.
So complaint yourself to find the
Solution of the problem,
What you do to take out best from
Them.

30. Leftover

When a dream end,
A superstar lost her stage,
A bond is going to break.
When life becomes a dream
And your dream move to another
Dream,
In between the shifting everything
Switch,
The emotion of love that changes with
The small change,
Something that accelerates you is
Exhausting now.
Something that makes you take
Decision bounded and unreasonable,
Being a different person with different
Personality,
When you leave your favourite person,
favourite cloth, Favourite pet
In all these changes everything change
But the feeling of sepration and it's
Pain lefts.

31. Home

When a child leaves his home
and Move to study,
When a soldier leaves his home
to Serve the army to his country,
When a girl leaves her home for
Her husband,
When a man leaves home
that have wife and
Children to work,
When a girl leaves her home
of childhood to become a lady,
When a boy leaves her home
of childhood To come to a man,
When a man leaves the home of his heart
of a woman
When your ex reminds his home
of heart that You leave,
When a child leaves home
of money of their
Parents and start a new life,
Your home will always miss you!!!

32. Child in me

I love the time of life
When we read stories
of old time.
The greatest nostalgia I am
Finding into me.
When some beautiful rhyme
Rewind in my mind,
Gestures and feeling of lying
Under falling autumn leaves,
The feeling that let you loose
Your anxiety,
Caramel and sour tamarind time.
I remember the moment
when I love everything about mine.
When life has nothing to deal
With, two cousins watching a movie
With faces that grin
A cute mom awaking me after ten
The moment in which I dance without
Hesitation.

There is nothing that worries me

That is the ten-year-old girl in me still
Recapping memories that she feels.
I love that child that was left in me.

33. Perry

I carry spectacles on
my nose,
Watching film with me.
My spectacle name
is perry,
i m having an Amazing
grip with the stick
of perry.
We watch movie together,
We love same character that
Are clever.
Perry see the darkest
night with me
He knew the childhood
in me
He know all the weakness
apart still
Holding and sitting
over my nose
With my crazy scars.
They knew how i
see this world

The focus of my eye,
They remember
every blink,
beautiful dresses i
see in the market.
And Make eyes feel
humble from inside.

My peery know when
i use to cry
In my saddest part
and scars that i gave
To eyes.

Sometimes perry feel sick
when he is In my drawer,
He don't like me when
I wear lenses in my eyes.
Whenever i forgot him
I found this world so blur,
It's like my life is a low
quality graphics Picture.
My perry always by my side
My ornaments for all the times.

34. Bucket

This is my empty bucket of
Life,
Let's pour some life into life.
Tiring typical and no one to
Honour,
Getting something lets you first
Pay a lot.
There is too much traffic in my mind
About people and their thoughts,
Tapping down from my cloud
Into reality in proud,
But life here is so loud,
Every place is covered by a crowd.
Bouquet has beautiful flowers
With a feeling of heaven's door,
But still, it can not fill the life pores.
Extremely choosy and favourable
Life,
But sometimes it brings tears to my
Eyes,
Still, life is a bunch of surprise.

35. Expectations

Expectations from unclear efforts,
The fighter in you fights for more.
Confused minds have their
own dilemma,
But freaky minds have no cure
Pulling out life from unlived parts
Baggage of age and society,
Keep you in war.
Lifting humour, fighting from
Warrior,
Quater parts of yours are
Uncomplete and uncherished.
Creepy fingers have no notes
Bundle to count,
Money changes everything in
One ounce.
But more than money something
Else that kill,
False expectations make fuzzy films
And in the last, they spoil your confidence
To make awkward,
And lead you towards your graveyard.

36. Selflove

When you are pleasing
To effort more,
When you are waiting for
The next surprise to explore
When you are a good-hearted
Innocent child,
but your feelings die for a
Smile.
Then you need to find more,
You have to use your energy to
Know,
Exercising and burning your day
For love is an extraordinary way,
Write a short note to yourself,
Wakeup and enjoy each and
everyday.

37. Better days

Feelings are deep like well,
You have no time left to kill.
Crazy opinions don't matter
So just sell,
Maybe one day with my daughter
I am playing with sea-shell.
Hazy hair like a black cloud
On my face,
I am just waiting for a beautiful
Rain.
What it feels when the bright turn
Into dark days,
What if all the eyes are on you
And you are depressed.
Your careless gesture vanish
All your opportunities,
And every day becomes a hard day
There is a never Ending
expectations on the back,
That fades all the colours
into grey.

Now only the next rain can save me
From this blames,
Spending days in the hope of better
Days.

38. Days

Good moments are hard to
Take place,
Even bad things are easily
happening Every next day,
These days You are
willing to take the stress.
I have a simple query to ask,
Why it is hard to think above
The faith that you built,
Even you know this is not the
Truth.
Still, the person in you is afraid
Of building the life under the
pool,
you know water follows the path
of Nasal cavity and reach into
your roots.
And you know you will die very
soon.
Your hard work, luck and past
experience Are worrying about
your life and literal

Lovers standing near your soul.
Your death is an experience that you
never Suppose to be true,
that unwanted silence knocking
Your door,
And suddenly you realise this life is
About something more, that you never
Know.

Thank you so much for reading this book

• 63 •